AF371544

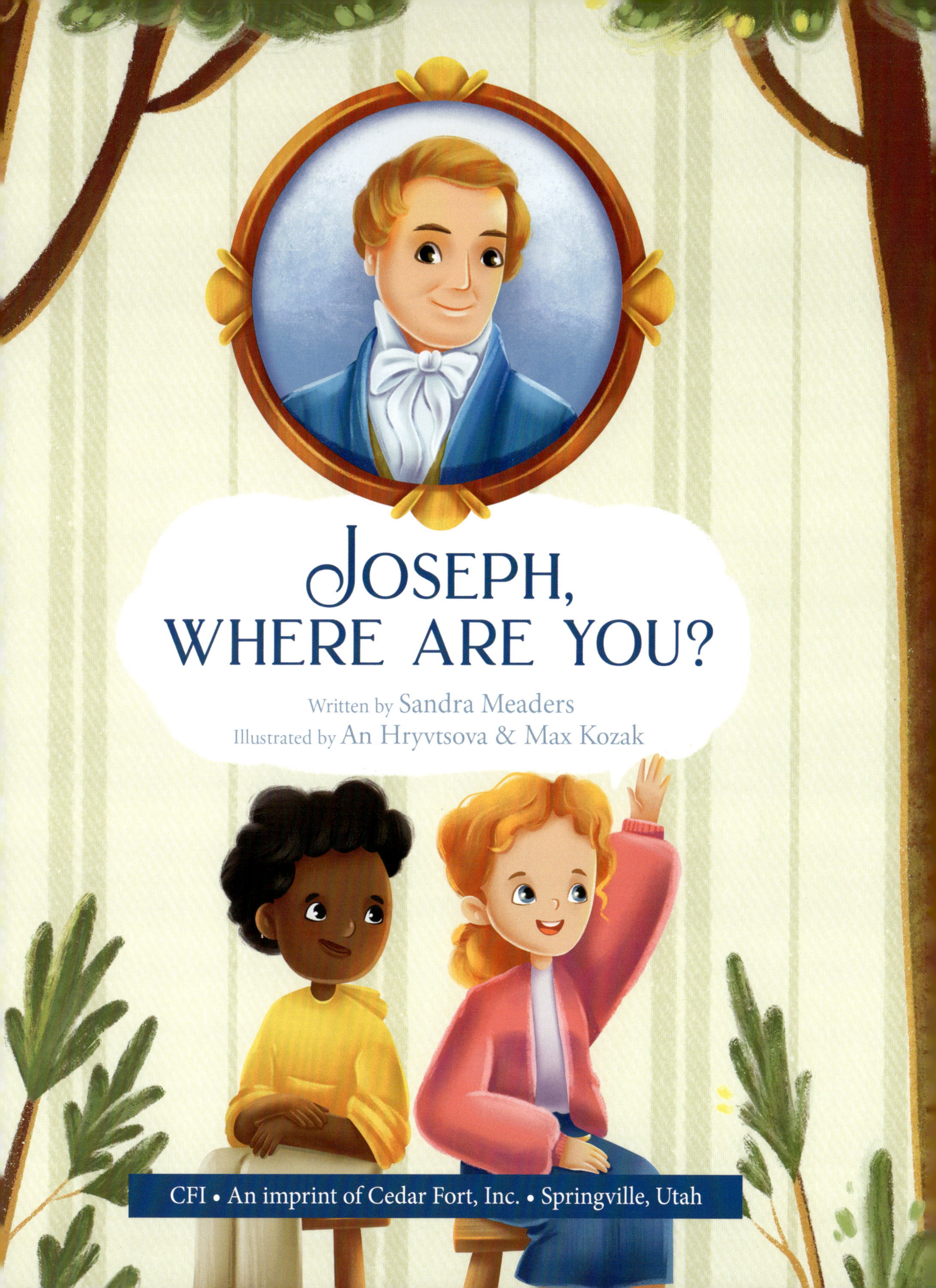

Joseph, Where Are You?

Written by Sandra Meaders

Illustrated by An Hryvtsova & Max Kozak

CFI • An imprint of Cedar Fort, Inc. • Springville, Utah

This book is dedicated to
James D. Meaders, my kids (Henry,
Eleanor, and Willoughby), Melanie Meaders,
Kathleen Gwilliam, Dr. Paul Reeves, and
the heroes represented in this book.

—Sandra

ISBN 13: 978-1-4621-4845-5

Published by CFI, an imprint of Cedar Fort, Inc.
2373 W. 700 S., Suite 100, Springville, UT 84663
Distributed by Cedar Fort, Inc., www.cedarfort.com

Library of Congress Control Number: 2024942988

Cover design and interior layout and design by Shawnda T. Craig
Cover design © 2024 Cedar Fort, Inc.

Printed in China

10 9 8 7 6 5 4 3 2 1

Printed on acid-free paper

Welcome to Primary!

Joseph Smith, Jr. had a question and looked for the answer in the Bible. He read the verse, "If any of you lack wisdom, let him ask of God."

Joseph, where are you?

I am in the Sacred Grove near Palmyra, New York. I pray to ask God which church is true. Heavenly Father and Jesus appear to me.

Moroni, an ancient Book of Mormon prophet, kept the records of his people and hid them, so they wouldn't be lost and could be read later.

Moroni, where are you?

I am on the Hill Cumorah to show Joseph where the gold plates were buried. Joseph will translate the plates into the Book of Mormon.

Oliver Cowdery, a school teacher,
helped Joseph by writing down Joseph's
translation of the Book of Mormon.

Oliver, where are you?

I am at the Susquehanna River. Peter, James, and John appeared to us and gave us the priesthood and authority to baptize. I will baptize Joseph, and he will baptize me.

Elijah Abel was one of the first black men
to receive the Melchizedek priesthood.
As a faithful member, Elijah worked as a
seventy and went on three missions.

Elijah, where are you?

I am at the
Kirtland Temple.

I helped build it and I participate often in the temple ceremonies to learn more about God. I received my washing and anointings here.

Emma, Joseph Smith's wife, stood by her husband even when people tried to harm them or made fun of them for their beliefs. She took care of Joseph when an angry mob hurt him, and followed him from place to place as the Saints looked for a place to call home.

Emma, where are you?

I am at the Red Brick Store in Nauvoo, Illinois.
I am called to preside over a new organization
of women to help and serve. It's called the
Relief Society that will someday be the largest
women's organization in the world. I am also
compiling a book of hymns that the saints will
use to sing and praise God.

Jane Elizabeth Manning learned about the Church in Connecticut and became a member of the Church of Jesus Christ of Latter-day Saints.

Jane, where are you?

I am in Winters Quarters, Nebraska.
I walked 800 miles to be with the saints
in Nauvoo. The Saints were driven out and
now we are preparing to go out west.

Brigham Young became the prophet after Joseph Smith died. The members of the Church worried for their safety. He prayed to the Lord for direction, and the Lord told him that the members of the Church needed to leave Nauvoo.

Brigham, where are you?

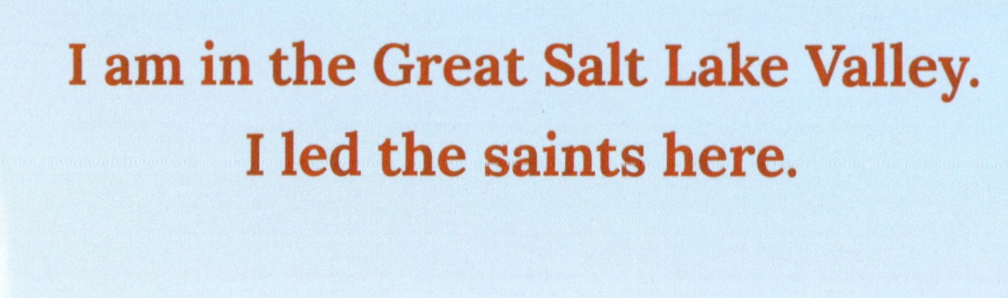

I am in the Great Salt Lake Valley.
I led the saints here.

I will help direct the members of the
Church to build homes across
the west and start building temples.